THIS WALKER BOOK BELONGS TO:

_____

_____

_____

_____

whippety willow

strips of hide

ribs of palm

liana vines

wriggly fish bone
skeleton

elephant grasses

sinuous twig

to string …
to tune, tense, key up,
thread, tie, hang, fasten,
arrange in a line,
provide with a string,
extend, s-t-r-e-t-c-h,
tease …

bulrushes

For John and Anna with love
J.H.

For Anne Veronica with love
M.C.

First published 1993 by Walker Books Ltd
87 Vauxhall Walk, London SE11 5HJ

This edition published 2001

2 4 6 8 10 9 7 5 3 1

Text © 1993 Judy Hindley
Illustrations © 1993 Margaret Chamberlain

This book was typeset in Garamond

Printed in Hong Kong

British Library Cataloguing in Publication Data:
a catalogue record for this book is available
from the British Library

ISBN 0-7445-8208-3

A Piece of String

is a wonderful thing

Judy Hindley   illustrated by Margaret Chamberlain

WALKER BOOKS
AND SUBSIDIARIES
LONDON · BOSTON · SYDNEY

Let us sing a song
about string –
what a wonderful thing it is!
When you think of the things
that you do with string,
you have to admit
it's a marvellous bit
to have in your kit:

My friend's uncle said, "You should never go anywhere without a coin for a phone box, a pencil stub and a piece of string."

for a fishing line, a boat, a kite,
somewhere to hang your socks to dry;
for tying up parcels, fastening gates,
leading you safe through a treacherous cave;
for a spinning-top, a skipping-rope,
a bracelet, a necklace, a draw-string purse…
there's just about no end of things
a person can do with a piece of string!
And then you wonder,
from time to time,
how did a thing like
string begin?

← slip knot

A slip knot can hitch
a boat, a horse,
a swing…

three small knots

three big knots

three small knots

= ... _ _ _ ...
= Morse code for S.O.S.

7

Back in the days
when mammoths roamed,
and they didn't have chains
and they didn't have ropes
for hauling things round
or lifting them up –

The bodies of birds and animals are worked by living strings called sinews.

(well, they didn't have any connecting things:
buttons or braces or buckles or laces
or latches or catches or bolts or belts,
or tabs or clasps or hooks-and-eyes…
Velcro patches! ribbons! ties!
zips or grips or snaps or clips)
well how did anyone
THINK IT UP?

About 2.5 million years ago, people were chipping stones to make a cutting edge… but it took us 2 million years to get the edge sharp enough to cut out leather strips.

In New Guinea, people make fishing nets out of spiders' webs. They leave a wooden frame with a colony of spiders, who spin their webs around it. In the British Museum, I saw a spiders' web hat that was made this way.

Did they chat as they sat
round the fire at night,
eating their prehistoric fish,
and say, "What we need
to do it right
is a thing like hair,
but long and strong,
a thing to tie on a bit of bone:
what a wonderful fishing line
that would make!"?

After which, I suppose,
they went out to the lake
and tickled the fish
with their cold, bare hands –
for they didn't have nets
if they didn't have string.
How they all must have wished
that they had such a thing!

For a long time the only spears were pointed sticks.
Much later, a chip of stone would be tied to
the stick with a sinew.

So how on earth
do you think they discovered it?
Do you think somebody
just tripped over it?
Was it an accident?
Was it a guess?
Did it emerge
from a hideous mess?
Did it begin with
a sinuous twig,
a whippety willow,
a snaky vine…?

In order to hunt successfully, people had to start working as a team. But there's always a slowcoach …

12

Did it happen that somebody, one dark night,
wending his weary way home alone,
got tripped by the foot on a loop of a vine
and fell kersplat! and bust a bone;
and then, as he lay in the dark, so sad,
and yelled for help (and it didn't come)
he got thoroughly bored with doing that
and invented – a woolly-rhinoceros trap?

Teams of hunters drove their prey over cliffs...
or possibly into holes hidden by vines.

13

Oh, it might have occurred in a number of **ways**
as the populace pondered the fate they face**d –**
as they huddled in caves
in the worst of the weather,
wishing for things like
tents
and clothes,
as they hugged bits of fur
to their shivery bodies
and scraps of skins
to their cold, bare toes.

In time, ancient hunters learned to use sinews to string their bows.

" If only there was something to join our clothes together ..."

And they didn't have braces
or poppers or laces
or buttons or toggles
or grips or pins –
so HOW did they hold up their trousers, then?
They must have said,
"Oh! a piece of string
would be SUCH a fine thing
to have around the cave!"

The very first needles were probably thorns.

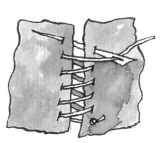

15

One hunting breakthrough was the bolas — three stones tied to a leather strap or a sinew. It was whirled round an animal's legs to trip it up.

Things on strings are a glamorous way to deck your body. Think of necklaces, pendants, belts and bracelets.

They needed a noose for an antelope foot.
They needed a thing to string a bow.
They needed nets, and traps, and snares
for snaffling rabbits unawares
and leading the first wild horses home…

Well, they must've gone on to try and try
as hundreds of thousands of years went by…
twisting and plaiting and trying out knots
with strips of hide and rhinoceros guts,
spiders' webs and liana vines,
reeds and weeds and ribs of palm,
slippery sinews, thews and thongs,
elephant grasses three feet long
and wriggly fish-bone skeletons…

fish trap   antler harpoon ~ a spear with a string attached   antler spearhead

And they spun out the fibres
of vegetable fluff
and they felted the hairs of a goat,
and they knitted and twisted
and plaited and twined …

A single fibre of wool is as strong as a thread of gold.

SPINNING A THIN THING FROM A FAT THING

Yarn is spun from sheep's fleece, cotton tufts or even birds' down.

Try spinning with cotton wool. Pull and stretch it very gently, very steadily, twisting it really tight as it draws out.

and invented …

TURNING A THIN THING INTO A FLAT THING

The next trick is weaving and knitting to make fabric…
Or tiny short hairs, laid down higgledy-piggledy,
wetted and pressed together, can be turned into felt.

the three-ply rope!
What a wonderful thing!
A very fine thing!
The KING of string
is rope!

Making Rope

One man twists two strands clockwise and walks forward.

A second man makes sure the strands of rope are laid tightly together.

A third man closes the strands by twisting this tool anticlockwise and walks backwards as the rope is formed.

The Egyptians made rope from bulrushes, camel hair and flax.

The oldest rope ever discovered came from a tomb in Egypt. It was made from flax 5000 years ago.

Sometimes rope was even made from women's hair.

You can lift up pots
from an echoing well with it,
fling it to make a bridge;
you can haul along hulking hunks
of stone for building a pyramid
(and they did).

measuring a field

using a plumb-line

making sure stone is flat

bringing water from the well

21

You can also halter and harness
your animal friends...

The first plough was probably just
a forked branch tied to an ox.

Our earliest picture of a sailing boat
is on a 3000-year-old Egyptian pot.

And then again, when life gets tough
and it's time to be moving along,
you can use it to lash your luggage fast
to a camel, a goat, a raft, a boat –
oh! a stringable thing
is the only thing
to have when you're afloat!

But they still
went on and on,
sticking and spinning
and looping and gluing
and tying and trying out
more and more types,
faster and faster
and possibly madder

early cart

The pontoon bridge was an
early bright idea. It began
with a row of boats
all roped together.

Roman crane

24

early gravity railway

Isambard Kingdom Brunel went up in a hot-air balloon to lay the first rope of the famous Clifton Suspension Bridge in Bristol.

early flying machine

Hot metal can be stretched into rails and cables, ropes and delicate wires.

for pulleys and ladders and hoses and bridges and fences and winches and wires and pipes.

25

Where on earth
have we got to now?
What would a town
ever do without string
and things that go stringing along?
Candlewicks, rackets and violins,
telephones, plumbing and railway lines,
things that fasten and fuse and fix
and click and stick and link…

Can you even begin
to count the ways
that things connect
with other things?
It could just about
scramble your brain!

And to think it began
(though we'll never know when)
with somebody choking
on elephant gristle,
or trying to chew
through the stem
of a thistle,
or just stumbling into
the thing!

Oh, what we've done
with a piece of string
is a marvellous thing,
an amazing thing –
some would say
a crazy thing!
And one of these days
I might just go away
and begin it
all over
again…

rope

swing

chain

Look up the pages to find out about these stringable things. Don't forget to look at both kinds of words:
this kind
and *this kind* .

ribbon

sewing thread

Wool

filament

harness

A note from the author

Judy Hindley says, "What really excited me about this book was finding out that human beings have been playing with simple inventions for *hundreds of thousands* of years! I loved finding out some of the things we've been up to during all that time, and Margaret's illustrations capture that inventiveness with enormous fun, liveliness – and beauty besides."

Violin strings

telephone wire

A note from the illustrator

Margaret Chamberlain says, "I was thrilled to get a chance to work on this exceptional book with Judy Hindley – we had lots of fun and laughs exploring the possibilities and wonders of the off-beat subject of string!"

goat hair

pipes

lead

NOTES FOR TEACHERS

The READ AND WONDER series is an innovative and versatile resource for reading, thinking and discovery. Each book invites children to become excited about a topic, see how varied information books can be, and want to find out more.

☞ **Reading aloud** The story form makes these books ideal for reading aloud – in their own right or as part of a cross-curricular topic, to a child or to a whole class. After you've introduced children to the books in this way, they can revisit and enjoy them again and again.

☞ **Shared reading** Big Book editions are available for several titles, so children can read along, discuss the topic, and comment on the different ways information is presented – to wonder together.

☞ **Group and guided reading** Children need to experience a range of reading materials. Information books like these help develop the skills of reading to learn, as part of learning to read. With the support of a reading group, children can become confident, flexible readers.

☞ **Paired reading** It's fun to take turns to read the information in the main text or captions. With a partner, children can explore the pages to satisfy their curiosity and build their understanding.

☞ **Individual reading** These books can be read for interest and pleasure by children at home and in school.

☞ **Research** Once children have been introduced to these books through reading aloud, they can use them for independent or group research, as part of a curricular topic.

☞ **Children's own writing** You can offer these books as strong models for children's own information writing. They can record their observations and findings about a topic, make field notes and sketches, and add extra snippets of information for the reader.

Above all, Read and Wonders are to be enjoyed, and encourage children to develop a lasting curiosity about the world they live in.

Sue Ellis, Centre for Language in Primary Education